ALL OUR COMMUNITIES

YOU'RE PART OF THE
WORLD COMMUNITY

BY THERESA EMMINIZER

Gareth Stevens
PUBLISHING

Please visit our website, www.garethstevens.com. For a free color catalog of all our high-quality books, call toll free 1-800-542-2595 or fax 1-877-542-2596.

Cataloging-in-Publication Data
Names: Emminizer, Theresa.
Title: You're part of the world community! / Theresa Emminizer.
Description: New York : Gareth Stevens Publishing, 2020. | Series: All our communities | Includes a glossary and index.
Identifiers: ISBN 9781538245491 (pbk.) | ISBN 9781538245514 (library bound) | ISBN 9781538245507(6 pack)
Subjects: LCSH: Communities–Juvenile literature. | Cultural pluralism–Juvenile literature.
Classification: LCC HM756.E463 2020 | DDC 307–dc23

Published in 2020 by
Gareth Stevens Publishing
111 East 14th Street, Suite 349
New York, NY 10003

Designer: Sarah Liddell
Editor: Theresa Emminizer

Photo credits: cover, p. 1 Hurst Photo/Shutterstock.com; background texture used throughout april70/Shutterstock.com; papercut texture used throughout Paladjai/Shutterstock.com; p. 5 Rawpixel.com/Shutterstock.com; pp. 7, 9 Robert Kneschke/Shutterstock.com; p. 11 Patrick Foto/Shutterstock.com; p. 13 Dmytro Zinkevych/Shutterstock.com; p. 15 Benjamin Clapp/Shutterstock.com; p. 17 Naypong Studio/Shutterstock.com; p. 19 135pixels/Shutterstock.com; p. 21 Samuel Borges Photography/Shutterstock.com.

Printed in the United States of America

Some of the images in this book illustrate individuals who are models. The depictions do not imply actual situations or events.

CPSIA compliance information: Batch #CW20GS: For further information contact Gareth Stevens, New York, New York at 1-800-542-2595.

CONTENTS

Boldface words appear in the glossary.

Many Countries, One World

Whether you speak English, Chinese, or Spanish, or whether you live in America, Africa, or Asia, you are part of the world community. All the people on Earth share the world and its **resources**. How can we work together as a community?

Your World Community

A community is a group of people living and working together. People within a community share common **goals**. What are some goals of your world community? We all need a healthy world to live in, clean water to drink, and food to eat.

Community Members

Everyone within the world community must work together to meet these needs and accomplish these goals. World leaders like the president and everyday people like you, your friends, and your neighbors are part of the world community. Everyone has a role, or part to play.

Where Do You Fit?

Earth is a big place. You might wonder how you could make a difference. But the things you say and do each day have the power to help make your world community better for everyone. A healthy world starts with you.

What Can You Do?

People produce a lot of trash. Where does it all go? Some is **buried** in the ground and some is washed into oceans. This is bad for the **environment** and can hurt animals. You can help by **limiting** the amount of trash you make and by recycling.

Save Electricity

Using **electricity** uses up **fossil fuels**. This is unhealthy for the environment. You can help by limiting how much electricity you use. Turn off lights and unplug things that are powered by electricity when you're not using them.

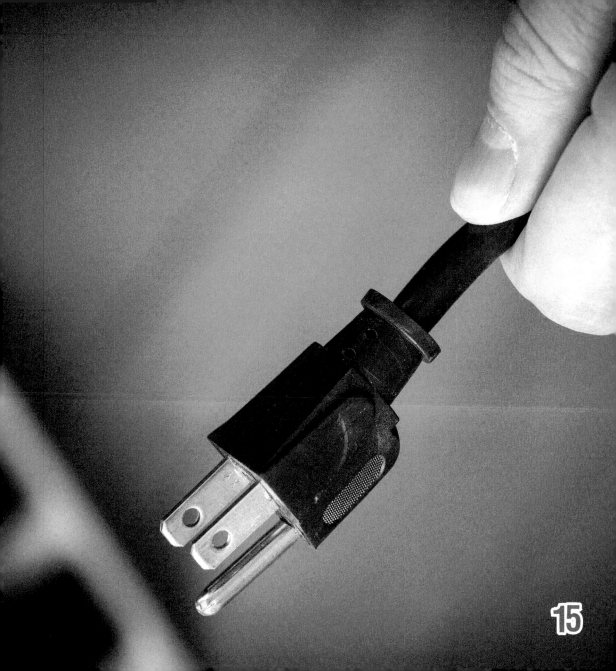

Conserve Water

Many people don't have clean, drinkable water. You can help by **conserving** water. Take shorter showers and turn off the tap when you brush your teeth. You could even catch rainwater in a bowl and use it to water plants.

Share What You Have

Food banks are places where hungry people in need can go to eat. You can gather canned goods and donate, or give them, to a food bank. Ask your parents if there is any extra food in your home that you could share.

We're All Neighbors

There are more than 7.7 billion people on Earth! We are all part of one world community. Together we can make Earth a healthy and happy place for everyone to live. It starts with you! Can you think of more ways to help?

GLOSSARY

buried: placed in the ground and covered

conserve: to save or not waste something

electricity: the flow of electrical power

environment: the natural world around us

fossil fuel: matter formed over millions of years from plant and animal remains that is burned for power

goals: something important someone wants to do

limiting: doing something as little as possible

resource: a useable supply of something

FOR MORE INFORMATION

BOOKS

Boone, Mary. *I Can Care for Nature.* Mankato, MN: Capstone Press, 2019.

Nagle, Jeanne. *What Is a Community?* New York, NY: Britannica Educational Publishing, 2017.

WEBSITES

Britannica Kids
kids.britannica.com/kids/article/community/626292
Learn more about what it means to be part of a community.

Kids Go Global
kidsgoglobal.net/the-issues
Find out about problems in your world community and how you can help solve them.

INDEX